A PURPOSE FOR PATCHES

A PURPOSE FOR PATCHES

A STORY OF COMPASSION FOR OTHERS AND LEARNING SURVIVAL SIGNS AND TOOLS.

GAIL L. OXFORD
ILLUSTRATOR: MELISSA FOX

Text and Illustrations copyright © 2023 Gail Oxford

Published by Purposeful Pals LLC

All rights reserved. No part of this publication may be reproduced, distributed, or transmitted in any form or by any means, including photocopying, recording, or other electronic or mechanical methods, without the prior written permission of the publisher, except in the case of brief quotations embodied in reviews and certain other noncommercial uses permitted by copyright law.

The moral right of the author and illustrator has been asserted.

Cover design and illustrations by Melissa Fox

Hardback ISBN-13: 979-8-89109-122-1
Paperback ISBN-13: 979-8-89109-120-7
eBook ISBN-13: 979-8-89109-121-4

Oxford, Gail

A Purpose for Patches / Gail Oxford

A Purpose for Patches follows the journey of a guide dog in training named Patches, who learns survival signals to assist his blind future owner, Sam, in navigating the city safely. All he wants is to fulfill his purpose and accompany Sam as his loyal guide. Will Patches complete his training and graduate?

Learning about signals and signs supports social studies standards for young learners. Children are able to watch for street signs and signals just like Patches does for Sam in this colorful story!

To God—for Your Son, Jesus Christ, and Your never-ending love and guidance.

To my husband, children, grandchildren, and friends—Thank you for your understanding, honesty, support, and kindness, especially during this new venture of mine.

To all my students—Navigating the world is challenging for everyone, but being visually impaired and trying to navigate can make the world feel threatening, menacing, and perilous. Remember to believe in yourself; follow the signs.

Patches jumped on the bus with his classmates.
Excitement filled the air as they
wagged their tails and found their seats.

Patches and the other dogs were finishing their basic training. Today they were going to learn important survival signs. If Patches passed his test, he would go home with his own special child, Sam, who was born blind.

The bus rumbled down the road. Patches sniffed the air and enjoyed the sights. Suddenly the bus screeched to a stop! Patches peered out the window with his keen eyes. He saw a big **red** sign with white letters that spelled STOP.

His teacher, Mrs. Gruff, said, "This is a stop sign." Patches knew when he took Sam on a walk, he would stop when he saw this sign.

The bus lurched forward and rattled down the road. Patches gazed out the window at a **black** rectangular box hanging from a metal bar in the middle of the road. He saw three colored lights; **red**, **yellow**, and **green**. The bus slowed down as the **yellow** light got brighter.

"That's a traffic light," Mrs. Gruff pointed out. 'It's your job to know what the colors stand for." Patches and his friends sat very still to listen. "NEVER take your human across an intersection when the light turns **yellow** or **green**," she added.

The light turned **red** and the bus stopped. Patches looked at his teacher, barked rapidly, and wagged his tail. Mrs. Gruff laughed and said, "That's right Patches, **red** means stop." Patches knew being cautious was his job in keeping Sam safe.

A loud siren blared as an ambulance raced down the road. Patches saw a big **blue** and white sign with a giant H.

Mrs. Gruff said, "This sign shows the way to the hospital, where doctors and nurses take care of sick and hurting people."
If Sam got hurt, Patches would find this sign to get Sam to help quickly!

The bus came to a stop. Mrs. Gruff pointed to the sign above the door, which spelled **EXIT**. She said, "This sign shows the way to safely leave a bus or building."

Patches and his classmates walked slowly and carefully toward the sign and got off the bus.

The pups followed Mrs. Gruff to a street corner. They saw a sign with a **red** flashing hand and heard a beeping sound. She said, "That means we have to wait to cross the street."

Patches stared at the **red** flashing 🛑. The light changed to **white** in the shape of a person walking 🚶. Mrs. Gruff said, "We may cross the street now." Patches understood how important these signs were to keep Sam safe.

After they crossed the street, Mrs. Gruff took them to a building where they saw signs on two doors. Mrs. Gruff said, "It's important to know the symbols when you take your child to the restroom." Patches knew Sam was a boy and understood which door he would take Sam to.

The dogs scurried to get some treats. Right in their path was a large container. On it was a skull with crossbones and the word DANGER.

Mrs. Gruff warned them to stay away. "That is POISON!" Patches and his friends made sure to walk around it. Patches would remember that he needed to protect Sam and keep him away from anything with these words on it!

The group finally arrived at Pawsitive Vibes Pet Shop and selected their treats. Mrs. Gruff paid for them and thanked the sales clerk. Patches and his friends yapped a heartfelt thank you and followed their teacher out the door.

As the pups strolled down the sidewalk, they immediately saw another **red** sign. It had a white cross on it. It was a FIRST AID STATION.

Patches knew that if Sam took him for treats at Pawsitive Vibes and got hurt along the way, this was a close place to take him for help.

As they continued down the sidewalk, a policewoman with a German Shepherd came towards them. "I'm so proud of your hard work and dedication to keeping people safe," she told them. "**Police** are here to protect and serve, just like guide dogs! You can always come to me or someone dressed in this uniform if you need help." They raised their paws to shake her hand and bowed their heads to Sarge, the German Shepherd.

They proceeded down the street and rounded the corner. A big **red** fire station and a Dalmatian were right in front of them. They barked excitedly at seeing another dog.

The Dalmatian, Dotty, loped up to them with a fireman right behind her. Dotty circled and wagged her tail. Patches politely shared his treats with Dotty. She graciously gave them a firehouse tour while Mrs. Gruff and the fireman chatted.

It was getting late. Mrs. Gruff needed to let the secretary know they were heading to school, but she had forgotten her phone. Patches spotted a cell phone on the desk beside the fireman. He pushed it with his paw toward Mrs. Gruff. She exclaimed, "Oh, Patches, you are doing wonderful at learning signs and finding ways to help Sam!" Mrs. Gruff politely asked the fireman if she could use the cell phone.

The fireman gave them directions and they headed down the street to catch their bus. Patches barked and pointed with his paw to a rectangular **blue** and white sign with the symbol of a bus. Patches demonstrated that he knew his signs!

After a long ride back, Patches and his classmates arrived at school.
A big **yellow** sign with an outline of children walking on it was placed in the street—Patches knew he could safely cross the street in the crosswalk. The young guide dogs were greeted by their parents with a lot of yipping and yapping as they shared their fantastic adventure of learning.

After two more weeks of training, Patches took his test and passed! Patches started counting the days until
he would get to live with Sam.

Finally, the day Patches had been waiting for arrived. Sam presented Patches with his diploma. They both hugged and jumped for joy! Sam got his dog and Patches got his very own boy.

Patches had a purpose; he was now an official service dog!

ABOUT THE AUTHOR

For forty-five years, Gail Oxford dedicated her life to education, ranging from being a first-grade teacher to a special education director (TOA) in Arizona. She has been heard many times stating, "Teaching is a passion, not a job!"

In her downtime, Gail can often be found outdoors enjoying her love for nature and being among the animals. Her adventurous side has her fishing, hiking, snowmobiling, 4-wheeling, horseback riding, and white-water rafting.

Gail always had a strong desire to write a book of her own, especially a children's picture book. Having worked with some amazing kids in special education, she was inspired to enlighten the world and normalize para-abilities and neurodiversity her debut through her writing. In this manner, *A Purpose for Patches* was born—children's book, with many more to come!

ABOUT THE ILLUSTRATOR

Melissa Fox has always loved paper, scissors, color, and art. As a certified teacher for 40 years, she has enjoyed guiding children to express their imagination and creativity through various mediums.

Whether she is within the classroom walls or exploring world cultures, Melissa continues to look at art through the eyes of a child, by noticing the color, shape, and passion of the creator.

ACKNOWLEDGMENTS

I give Almighty **God**, the praise, glory, and thanks for **His** grace, mercy, and blessings throughout my life. **He** has given me all that I have and without **Him** I am nothing.

My loving, wonderful, and devoted husband, **Jack.** He has definitely been my pillar of support and strength. I wrote my book six years ago and placed it in my cowboy boot box. He encouraged me to dig it out and spurred me to get it published. **Jack**, you have been my sounding board by listening to my countless reads and re-reads and answering my numerous questions as to, "Should I change the word to this…, does this sound better? "Thank you so much *my love* for always being there for me."

Melissa Fox, my precious, treasured, true, and dear friend; you have been a sister to me all of these years. Thank you for your empathy, love, support, and great sense of humor. I am grateful for your exceptional creativity with your illustrations for my book, and lastly, your extreme patience and understanding for all of the editing changes that were made!

Marcy Pusey, my chief editor. Where do I begin…I have so much to thank you for! There are not enough words to express and demonstrate my deep and sincere gratitude to you. You have provided me with invaluable guidance and encouragement throughout the process of perfecting my book. Your expertise and advice have clearly been exceptional. I am so grateful you accepted my request to be my editor!

Creative and talented editor, **Mandi Summit**. Thank you for your creativity, positive energy, exemplary word choice, and figurative language suggestions. You gave me the inspiration to create a more colorful and playful children's book.

Thank you to all of my **dear and cherished treasures; my students**. You have given me such joy and I have learned so much from you. You have inspired me and have assisted me as an educator and author. Because of You, teaching became my passion, not a job!

Last, but not least, **Chandler Bolt** and his **team** at selfpublishing.com, thank you for your support, encouragement, continual communication, coaches, training, videos, sessions, expertise, and always checking on me to keep me on track!

www.ingramcontent.com/pod-product-compliance
Lightning Source LLC
Chambersburg PA
CBHW061349010526
44107CB00011B/876